"I Remember Normanby..."

Life on a Lincolnshire Estate Between the Wars

Compiled by
David J. Taylor

Scunthorpe Museums &
The Hutton Press
1994

Published by Scunthorpe Museums
and the Hutton Press Ltd.,

130 Canada Drive, Cherry Burton, Beverley,
North Humberside HU17 7SB

Typeset and printed by
Image Colourprint Ltd.,
Willerby, Hull.

ISBN 1 872167 62 4

CONTENTS

INTRODUCTION

This book chronicles the life and times of Normanby Hall and the Normanby Estate in the first half of the 20th Century. During that period Normanby, like many English country houses, experienced its final Indian Summer before the dramatic social upheavals that took place after the Second World War. In those days, however, the Hall was still the home of the Sheffield family, was still surrounded by large estates, and was still the focus of a community. Moreover, the traditional country house style of living, that would have been recognisable to someone alive a hundred years earlier, also remained intact. Much has since changed but it is hoped that something of the flavour of this way of life has been recaptured in this account.

These changes affected Normanby. In 1949 Sir Berkeley Sheffield's immense servants' wing was demolished and fourteen years later the Hall and Park were leased to Scunthorpe Borough Council. Thus the Sheffield family, who have owned Normanby since the 16th century, ceased to live there for the first time in centuries. But in a period of uncertainty this was a far happier outcome than the fate which befell other stately mansions. It has been estimated that since 1945 some 600 country houses have been demolished in Great Britain.

After the leasing of the Hall and Park to Scunthorpe Borough Council it became part of the Council's Museum Service and displays were created that primarily featured decorative and fine art and emphasised its Regency period origins. Over the years, however, it had become apparent that an essential part of the Hall's history was being lost - the experience of what it was like to live and work at Normanby. What better way of recalling these lost years than through the words of those who had lived through them? Consequently, between 1992 and 1993 an oral history project was undertaken which eventually led to the taping of 39 interviews with local people who had known the Hall and Estate in its heyday.

The people interviewed ranged from a former head housemaid to the son of a head chauffeur, a head gardener, a kitchenmaid and soldiers based at Normanby during the Second World War. All had fascinating stories to tell and both their generosity in allowing their reminiscences to be recorded for posterity and their hospitality were much appreciated. Inevitably the majority of their memories were from the first fifty years of the 20th century but material from before and after that period was also collected.

This book is essentially a distillation of these recordings and it includes quotations where appropriate, some of which have been slightly edited for the benefit of the reader. So much material was gathered by the project that it has been impossible to include it all and apologies are therefore offered for omissions.

Above all this is the story of Normanby Hall as told by the domestic staff who lived in the old servants' quarters, the gardeners who worked in the Park, the bricklayers and joiners from the old Estate Yard, the gamekeepers on the Estate, and the tenants who lived in the local villages. It is their story told in their own words, and it unlocks the secrets of a local example of that most complex of institutions, the English country house.

BELOW STAIRS

Between 1905 and 1907 Sir Berkeley Sheffield employed a York architect called Walter Brierley to extend his country seat. He designed an elegant new east wing in 'classical baroque' style as well as large domestic servants' quarters. The former still stands, but the servants' wing was demolished in 1949, surviving for less than fifty years. Following the usual practice it was built on the colder, north side of the Hall and replaced an earlier wing. Few photographs show it clearly as it was screened, as was customary, by shrubs and trees but this immense three storey red brick wing rivalled the Hall itself in size.

The new service wing was modern and well-appointed for the time and created a lasting impression on the people who lived there. It had central heating, electric lighting, bathrooms and toilets - amenities only dreamt of in the homes of nearby villagers. Nevertheless, all the bedrooms still possessed fireplaces. The ground floor contained the main working areas, the butler's pantry, housekeeper's room, kitchen, scullery, servants' hall, still-room and various larders. Above were the female staff's bedrooms on the first floor and the men's on the floor above. Servants entered the wing from the north, where they passed through an open wooden courtyard around which were a single-storey bakehouse, brushroom, pumproom, toilets and a coalstore.

'As you went into the servants' hall, immediately on the right and left were the staircases on to the first and second floors. Immediately on the left on the ground floor was the kitchen, the big kitchen and the scullery combined. Then you went up a second flight of about six stairs, big stone stairs. At the top of these stairs on the left was the butler's pantry where all the silverware was kept religiously polished and cleaned, and beyond that a big pair of doors and you were virtually then on the verge of being in the Hall proper. Coming back on the other side, the first room on the opposite side was the housekeeper's apartments, then you had this long servants' hall.'

Although constructed in the Edwardian period the layout of the new wing followed the Victorian principle of dividing the ground floor into four zones according to use with a senior servant, namely the butler, cook, housekeeper and laundry-maid in charge of each. The exception at Normanby was the laundry area, as a separate one with its own cottage already existed in the Park. The other principle governing the design of the wing was the strict segregation of male and female staff with separate staircases leading to their bedrooms. One of the housemaids recalls:

'I knew there were ten rooms on each landing because I had them to polish! The top was the men's bedrooms and down below the women. There was a bathroom on each landing and there was also a toilet at the other end of the landing. They were all centrally heated; there were hot pipes running round them all. The head housemaid had her own room, and the lady's-maid and the housekeeper, and the second housemaid had her own room, but the third and fourth shared a room you see. And it was the same with the kitchen, the second kitchen-maid and scullery-maid had a *shared room.'*

Individual rooms were:

'beautiful. We each had a dressing table and a wash stand; of course you see there weren't bowls then like they have now, but we each had our own bowl and a jug of water to get washed and an easy chair.'

There were four grandfather clocks in the servants' wing and these were situated in the butler's pantry, the housekeeper's room, the servants' hall and the kitchen, as well as a plethora of clocks in the main Hall. Mr. Tate, a clock and watch maker from Winterton nicknamed 'Clocky', came to the Hall to wind them up every Saturday afternoon.

A young housemaid in the late 1930s also remembers the butler's pantry as a strictly male preserve:

'We couldn't go in there, we could go in to speak to them, but you weren't allowed to stop in there, clean the silver, all that.'

Most of the domestic staff lived in the servants' wing, with a few exceptions such as Lizzie Aldridge who came in to bake bread. The full complement numbered fifteen. These were a butler, two footmen, a hall-boy, cook, two kitchen-maids, a scullery-maid, a housekeeper, four housemaids, a lady's-maid, and an odd-man (so named because he did all the odd jobs). Household staff were either recruited informally in the locality by the housekeeper or even Lady Sheffield, or through 'respectable' servants'

agencies such as Mrs Massey's famous London agency. The number of servants employed in country houses declined markedly after the First World War, people often being replaced by labour-saving devices, but this does not appear to have happened at Normanby.

The housekeeper, who was always addressed as Mrs, whatever her age or marital status, was the most important female servant in the household, ranking above the cook and lady's-maid and on a par with the butler. She was in charge of the housemaids and the still-room and her duties were cleaning the house, looking after the linen and generally ensuring that the Hall ran smoothly and efficiently.

Each member of the staff stuck rigidly to his or her own tasks and it was rare for example, for housemaids to venture into the kitchen or kitchen staff to enter the house. There was an element of snobbishness in this although housemaids and kitchenmaids usually got on well together:

'Housemaids wouldn't look at cooking. They thought themselves that little bit better because they didn't get dirty, just worked through the front end of things.'

The Hall and the servants' quarters were in fact divided by the luggage entrance that serves as a rear entrance on the western side of the Hall today. Anything that needed taking directly into the Hall such as furniture passed through here. The lift shaft, a modern convenience for its time, was also located here and round it wound the servants' staircase. Household staff could usually be found rushing up and down these stairs as they went about their daily tasks, as they were in general forbidden to use the main stairway in the Hall.

The butler ruled over the two footmen, the hall-boy and the odd-man but was not responsible for valets. He was in charge of the plate, drink and table linen and also served at table. For this reason, the butler's pantry was the nearest room in the servants' wing to the dining room. It contained a large safe where all the silver was kept, including dining plates. The butler was also in charge of the beer and wine cellars. Butlers were married men and had a house in Normanby Village as well as a bedroom in the Hall if it was necessary for them to stay overnight.

One butler at the Hall between the Wars was Mr. Ashley. A Normanby villager remembers that as a boy,

'my first visits to the kitchens and servants' quarters at Normanby were under the auspices of Mr. Ashley who used to give us crystallised sugar on strings which was a great luxury.'

Another recalls him,

'because if you can remember Kensington cigarettes, Kensington cigarettes' advert was a butler with a silver salver and a packet of cigarettes on it, and Ashley was a typical butler, he looked exactly like the Kensington man.'

The servants' hall was the largest room in the old domestic wing, and it was here that most of the staff ate their meals:

'The servants' hall occupied quite a length of the building. There was nothing in there other than this very, very, big table surrounded by chairs of course. It was almost like a simple baronial hall as you would imagine it, a long heavy oak or solid wood table down the centre and big heavy chairs all the way round.'

Breakfast was at 8 a.m. (although the kichen staff always ate in the kitchen) and usually consisted of bacon and eggs, kedgeree, sausages, or sometimes porridge and cold ham. Lunch was a three course meal held at 12. 30 p.m.

'The butler used to sit at one end of the table and the housekeeper at the other. The butler served the meat, cut the meat off, and the housekeeper served the vegetables. The men sat down one side of the table, and the girls the other.'

The convention was observed whereby the housekeeper, the butler, the lady's-maid, and any visiting lady's-maids ate their main courses in the servants' hall, and then retired to the housekeeper's room or 'pugs' parlour' as it was more commonly known, to consume their sweet.

A housemaid recalls:

'When they'd finished their meat, whether I'd finished mine or not, I had to get up and open the door for them. They used to do a walking out, and the housekeeper especially used to have a tumbler of water in one hand and her bread on a fork in the other and go marching out. Then I used to have to take the pudding up to the housekeeper's , and the odd-man used to take the servants' hall meals in.'

This left the head housemaid to keep order in

the servants' hall. The ritual was only followed at lunchtime; tea and supper were taken separately by the senior servants in the 'pugs' parlour', waited on by the odd-man. Social functions were also held in the servants' hall such as an annual Christmas Servants' Ball to which all the estate workers were invited.

The cook was in charge of the kitchen and the scullery, which were situated to the rear of the servants' wing to avoid the smell of cooking in the main Hall. This was done on closed coal-fired cast-iron ranges, although later a large blue 'Aga' cooker was installed. A feature of the kitchen was rows of numbered polished copper moulds for making pies, creams and jellies.

'It looked tremendously big when you were in it. As you walked into the kitchen door it seemed to go far enough, all the ovens on the right, the old type, cast iron stoves. And sinks of various sorts, and all the racks with crockery on that seemed to stretch for far enough. Big huge tables in the centre where the food was prepared in the kitchen, then taken through to the next room to be properly laid out on the various salvers and what have you before it was served through the Hall.'

Food was cut up in the scullery behind the kitchen, which contained three large sinks, one solely for vegetables, and a marble-topped working surface in the centre.

'The table, the cook used to work there, and the first kitchen-maid opposite her and second kitchen-maid. And you never got in one another's way, so you know how big it was. Then of course the scullery-maid used to be at all the sinks ... the table used to be laid with knives and spoons and whisks, and of course there wasn't blenders, we used to have to use pestle and mortar for doing gelatines and that sort of thing.'

Most of the ingredients for the elaborate meals came from Normanby. Fruit and vegetables were grown in the large kitchen garden in the Park, the Home Farm was the source of meat and poultry, whilst game and rabbits were shot on the Estate. Milk and dairy produce came from a dairy farm worked by the Sheffields in Normanby Village. After the Second World War a pedigree herd of some 40 or so Jersey cows was kept there, producing rich cream and milk which became renowned throughout the district. In later years, meat was delivered from William Waite's butcher's shop in Burton Stather. Even bread, enough to feed the entire household, was baked by Lizzie Aldridge every Tuesday and Friday, sometimes with the help of the second kitchen-maid. This was in the bakehouse in the corner of the courtyard to the north of the servants' wing and is the only part that survives today.

A scullery-maid who began work in the kitchen in 1926 at the age of 16 on a wage of £23 a year remembers:

'Everything in those days came in raw you know. The chickens with all the feathers on just as they'd been killed. The pheasants, they had to be done from scratch. We used to pluck pheasants and chickens and skin rabbits. And an awful lot of washing up believe me ... The sinks were that big. They were copper, and you didn't have Fairy Liquid. You had soda, hot water and soda. By jove I've had some chapped hands in Winter believe *me, up to my elbows! Mind you, you weren't there long, you had to work that through to get a bit further up.'*

Apart from these duties her other main task was preparing vegetables for soups and stews. However she soon moved up to second kitchen-maid which allowed her to begin cooking meals for the staff. The cook and first kitchen-maid concentrated on meals served in the dining room.

Fish, meat and poultry were stored in four larders leading off the scullery and beyond them in the woods next to the servants' wing stood a latted wooden hut. This was for hanging game. Storing and preparing dry goods such as groceries, on the other hand, was the responsibility of the housekeeper. The kitchen staff also used ice-boxes lined with lead which were cooled by blocks of ice supplied by the fishmonger. The dome shaped ice-house in the grounds was built in 1817 as a means of storing ice but had become disused by this time. At one time it had been filled with ice cut by estate workers from the lakes in the Park.

The wonderful meals cooked in the kitchen would have done justice to any top class restaurant and in some ways it was a continuation of the aristocratic tradition of impressing guests not just with the quality of food provided, but also the quantity!

Household rubbish was removed each day in the following way:

'In the yard outside the servants' quarters there used to be a long hopper wagon; it tipped either way. Somebody, I don't know who, used to take this poor old donkey everyday, harness it up to this thing full of all the household rubbish and take it out and tip it, and bring it back empty. A daily trip for that poor old donkey.'

In the 1920s kitchen and house staff at the Hall had half a day off a week, and every other Sunday. They were expected to attend a morning service at St. Andrew's Church in Burton on their working Sundays.

If any of them wished to venture into Normanby Village,

'We used to have a little narrow walk, what they call 'servants' walk' at the side of the drive. We never walked up the drive.'

This ran between the southern wall of the kitchen garden and a hedge of rhododendrons, to a small wicket gate next to the main gate pillars. It was a way of ensuring the servants were kept out of sight of the gentry.

A second pathway ran from the gates to the gardeners' bothy on the north side of the kitchen garden. These gates, with their elaborate wrought ironwork, were made by the Burton village blacksmith Fred Drury in the 1930s, replacing a much simpler entrance.

Despite the hard work and discipline, downstairs life at the 'big house' in Normanby is remembered with warmth and affection, and the Hall as a 'homely place'. This was due in no small measure to the friendliness and kindly interest of the Sheffield family. The staff got on well together, and the experience of working at the Hall was regarded as good training for later on in life.

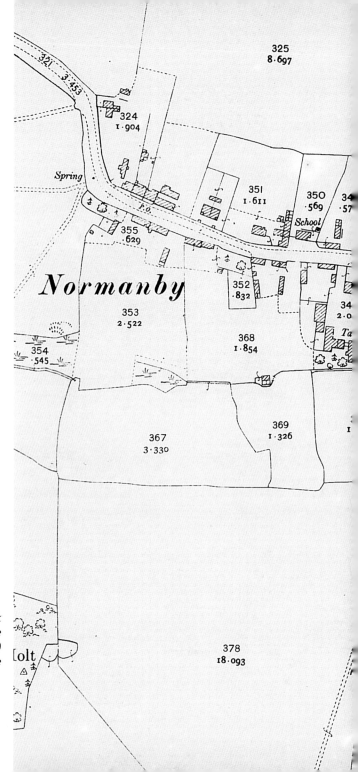

Map showing Normanby Hall, part of Normanby Park and Normanby Village in 1907, from the Ordnance Survey Second Edition, Lincolnshire (Parts of Lindsey) Sheet X.7. Reproduced with the permission of the Controller of H.M.S.O. (Crown Copyright).

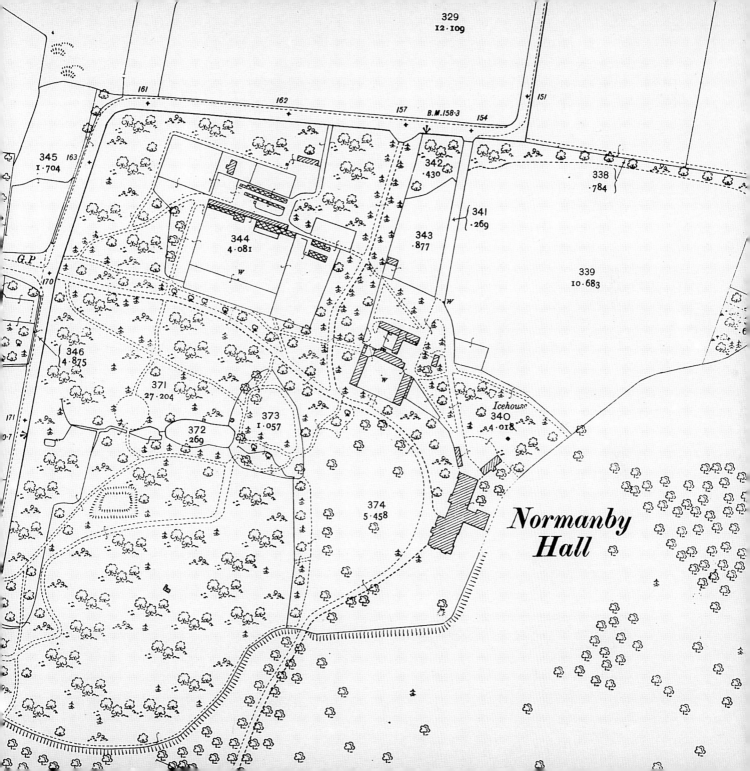

Normanby
Hall

Normanby Estate workers during the construction of the new servants' wing at the Hall taken by the Scunthorpe photographer, Arthur Henry Singleton.

Normanby Hall c.1910, with part of the former servants' wing visible on the left.

Snapshot of the front of the Hall in around 1937 with the servants' wing again just in view. It was taken by Leonard Newell when the family were not in residence.

The new domestic wing looking north from the luggage entrance, soon after it was constructed in 1907.

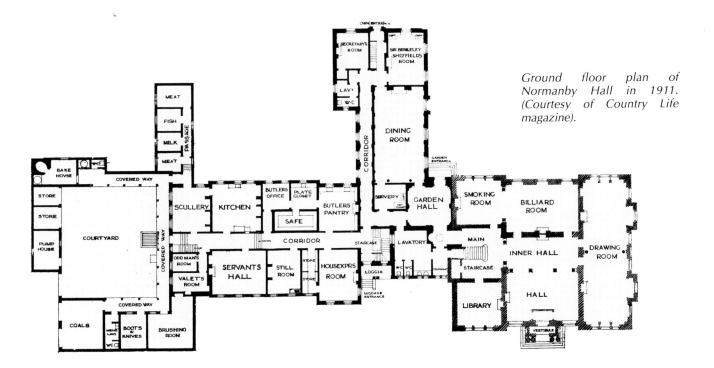

Ground floor plan of Normanby Hall in 1911. (Courtesy of Country Life magazine).

This is a view taken from behind the Hall looking at the recently completed servants' wing. It shows the single storey courtyard on the right and larders to the left.

14

The northern end of the new servants' wing taken from the courtyard . In this photograph the telephone lines have yet to be installed.

A very rare photograph of the interior of the servants' hall in the servants' wing during the First World War. Most of the group are convalescing soldiers.

Domestic staff taken behind the main Hall in the Summer of 1928 when the family were in London. The group is back row (left to right); Annie Campbell (2nd kitchen-maid), Maggie Dent (kennelmaid), Mrs. Williams (housekeeper), charwoman, Mary Camm (charwoman), Lizzie Aldridge (charwoman and breadmaker). Front row; housemaid, Ethel Drury (Head housemaid), housemaid.

Another group of domestic staff taken with some painters during Spring-cleaning in 1928. In the centre of the back row is the family butler, with a visiting chauffeur and a visiting butler on his right and left respectively.

16

The dining room during constrution in 1906 showing the original moulded ceiling, pillars and pilasters.

The dining room soon after construction.

Summer at Normanby c.1930. This view was taken by the Burton village photographer, Eric Wood.

The magnificent entrance hall in 1907.

18

The billiard room, again photographed in 1907. This room is situated immediately behind the main entrance hall.

Housemaids Mary Gunn and Lena Blanchard enjoy a game of leapfrog in the grounds of the Hall in 1937.

A 1937 photograph in the Park with Lena Blanchard on the left and Gladys Johnson, both housemaids at the Hall.

Lady Julia Sheffield's sitting room.

Detail of the fireplace in the drawing room.

Lady Julia Sheffield's sitting room.

The East Silk Drawing Room.

Corridor on the second floor of the east wing.

Lady Julia Sheffield's bedroom.

23

THE PARK

The focal point of Normanby Park was, and still is, the stableyard complex or 'courtyard' as it was sometimes referred to. This was designed by Sir Robert Smirke around 1820 before he commenced work on the Regency Hall, and its comparative opulence reflects the high status that horses afforded in those days.

By the 1920s, however, the west range was the only block in the yard still used to stable horses, including the individual mounts of Sir Berkeley Sheffield's children. A lady who grew up in Normanby Village and later worked at the Hall remembers that:

'The stables then, oh they were beautiful; we used to go with my father to take corn and that for the horses. I mean there used to be lovely horses in there ... they only had two or three horses when I was there, but I can still remember them having horses when I was a child, all the shopping was done with horses, but by the time I got to sixteen, they'd gone on to a van.'

As a result of the trend towards motorised transport the carriage house on the north side of the stableyard was converted into a garage capable of accommodating up to six large motor vehicles.

To the north of the garage block stood the gunroom, game-larder, laundry and a well equipped workshop. Here maintenance and repair work was carried out by the head chauffeur, and it also provided extra garage space if required.

Chauffeurs were a new type of country house servant created by the advance of technology, and there were two at Normanby. Both were on call 24 hours a day and a common trip was from Normanby to Doncaster station to meet the London trains. They also travelled abroad with the family. A somewhat less glamorous task was raking over the gravel in the stableyard!

The head chauffeur in the 1920s was Mr Frank Heritage, who moved up from Brighton and was with the Sheffield family for 27 years, marrying a housemaid called Lillian Fisher. The variety of luxurious cars he drove would bring tears of envy from any vintage car enthusiast. His son, who was born at Normanby, recalls that in the case of Sir Berkeley and Lady Sheffield:

'For many years they each ran a Rolls Royce, but latterly Lady Sheffield changed to a Lagonda. Sir Berkeley stuck religiously to Rolls Royces, although I remember one in particular was a sporty Rolls. It was a pale blue colour, had very upswept front mudguards. The registration number was 'GO 10', I've never forgotten that, and apparently he bought it from Sir Malcolm Campbell.'

(Sir Malcolm Campbell was a famous racing car driver who broke the land speed record on several occasions in the 1920s and '30s).

'The other members of the family, they would have cars like Invictas, or even again Rolls or Bentleys. I remember an Alvis being at Normanby Hall in the garage, and one of the sons at one time bought a big American car called an Albourne; I remember that one well, because it was a typical American car of the 1930s, like a gangster's car.'

The east range of the yard was originally built as stables and a carriage house but in the 1930s an underground petrol tank was laid close by. After the Second World War, an old Army ambulance was garaged there. This was used as an estate vehicle for transporting children from Burton School to local galas, by the Estate woodmen for carting logs to the Hall and by shooting parties. The stableyard was also the place where shooting parties congregated at 10.00 am before setting off for the day.

'There'd be an awful lot of activity in that stableyard. There'd be extra cars in, suddenly come in, they'd just park in the yard. And then there was always a big horse-drawn covered wagon, for bringing the game back in. There'd be quite big parties sometimes, we're talking of groups of twenty-five, thirty people trudging off for a day's shoot.'

Game shot on the Estate was hung in a building off the stable yard before being sent to the kitchen at the Hall. Behind it is a squash court built just before the Second World War but not used until after the conflict. The story goes that Sir Berkeley Sheffield's youngest son, John Sheffield, began his career in the construction industry by asking his father if he would like a squash court in the grounds of the Hall. While his father deliberated he went ahead and erected it then proceeding to present the bill to a none-too-pleased Sir Berkeley!

Also close by is Normanby Park Laundry where at one time all the the washing and laundering for the Hall was undertaken. It was built by the Estate but fell out of use after the First World War when the cheaper alternative of sending washing out was adopted and Mrs Gaunt in Alkborough took over the Hall's laundry work. The former head house-maid at the Hall in the 1930s remembers,

'I came across this girl, a long time ago now, who said she had learned to iron, ironing my print frocks; we all had to put our name on you see. We used to have to wear print frocks in the morning and white aprons, and in the afternoon we had to wear black.'

Next door is Laundry Cottage which was constructed early this century as accommodation for the laundry-maids. Fanny Aldridge and Polly Wilson were the last laundry-maids to live there and it was converted into living quarters for the head chauffeur and his family in the 1930s.

Another important section of the stableyard was an engine house where the fire engine operated by Normanby Park Fire Brigade was kept. A Brigade existed at Normanby until the beginning of the Second World War and next door to the engine house was a dressing room in which their uniforms, helmets and fire-fighting equipment was stored.

'I can still picture the fire engine itself in the station, and the room to the left with all these suits hanging, jackets and trousers, and big heavy boots and big brass helmets, silver one for the chief and brass ones for the crew. I can still see that as clearly if it was yesterday.'

The fire engine was a Shand Mason horse-drawn steamer built in 1900, but purchased second hand for the estate in 1915. Between then and the beginning of the Second World War it was the main means of fighting fire, not just at the Hall, but also in neighbouring villages, Scunthorpe being the nearest Municipal Fire Brigade. Happily, it was used in earnest on just one occasion in living memory, when it was called out to a stack fire at a farm in Thealby in 1939.

'I remember the men all running down from Normanby Village and diving into the building there at the bottom corner of the yard, putting all those heavy Navy blue coats on and big brass helmets and dashing off down that Thealby Drive.'

Their efforts were un-necessary, however, as Scunthorpe Fire Brigade had arrived before them and it was decided that the time had come to disband the Brigade.

Despite the rather antiquated appearance of the fire engine, to some local inhabitants Normanby Park Fire Brigade was a serious affair with a company of firemen made up of estate workers living in Normanby Village. When a warning of a fire was received it was the job of the youngest and fittest of the Normanby Estate Yard apprentices to run down to the station, open it up and light the fire in the engine. This ensured that it would be ready to pump when it reached the scene of the emergency. All the equipment was maintained in good working order and in the late 1930s an apprentice joiner used to,

'make sure that the fire was lit probably once a week to keep all the uniforms aired and make sure that the pumps and everything on the fire engine worked all right. Make sure the fire was laid to light it, because you had to light a fire for steam to work the pumps.'

The engine was capable of shooting a jet of water over the top of the Hall and representatives from Merryweather's, the fire engine manufacturers, came to drill the Brigade every year. Hoses were tested more frequently and this exercise was sometimes used as an excuse to pump out blocked drains on the Estate. The gardeners were responsible for looking after the hydrants in the House and grounds which were tested every fortnight. The Brigade also organised fire drills at the Hall, rescuing staff from upstairs windows by means of a sling. After the War, the steamer was occasionally brought out of store as a children's amusement at garden parties held in the grounds of the Hall.

Maintaining the 300 or so acres of grounds and gardens surrounding Normanby Hall in good condition was mainly the responsibility of the head gardener. He looked after the kitchen and pleasure gardens, but the Deer Park and wooded areas came under the aegis of the head woodman and his staff.

The head gardener was usually a married man, and lived in the first cottage on the right on the road to Burton in Normanby Village. He was an important figure in the running of the Estate, ranking alongside the clerk of works, the head gamekeeper and the head woodman in seniority. This importance was sufficient for him to have his name listed in Kelly's commercial directory for Lincolnshire.

In the mid-1930s he had a staff of seven, including four single men who lived in a bothy in the Park. These men were learning their profession at the Hall and a member of the house staff went in to cook for them at the bothy. Gardeners employed on country estates would travel to all parts of Britain as they moved from job to job, answering advertisements in journals such as the 'Gardeners' Chronicle'.

There were far more at Normanby in the 19th Century however, when numbers of estate workers in general greatly increased.

'There used to be twenty eight gardeners. When my uncle was eight years old he used to come to Normanby to scrub plant pots. He used to get 3d on Saturday morning for scrubbing plant pots.'

The large kitchen garden with apple trees and raspberries growing up its high walls was the hub of the gardens. It was built in 1817 and was the source of vegetables, plants and flowers for the Hall and even on occasions provided flowers for official ceremonies in Scunthorpe such as the opening of a new Post Office in 1939. It was approximately 200 yards long with a range of greenhouses running down the entire length of one side heated by two boilers. Produce cultivated in the green houses included vegetables and fruit grown out of season, as well as exotic fruit such as grapes, melons, nectarines and peaches. Vegetables from the kitchen garden were sent to the Hall on a daily basis.

'There was quite a lot of vegetables went up there. You used to send the apprentice every morning to the kitchen, you'd get a list of what vegetables they wanted and take them up there.'

In the case of flowers, the head gardener and one of his men went to the Hall, where there was a separate flower room, at 7 o'clock every morning before breakfast. Here they arranged the flower displays, putting on overshoes to avoid marking the carpets before taking them into the Hall.

The head gardener in the mid-1930s was enthusiastic about greenhouse work, and he recalls,

'Well I suppose one thing, in bad weather you was nice and warm! That's where all your work started from, even growing early vegetables. We used to have heated frames for growing early vegetables, carrots and lettuce, sea kale, rhubarb, all that sort of thing.'

He was also a carnation expert and started two carnation houses,

'Nothing else was grown in them and if you brought a new plant in, it was always isolated in case there was red spider, anything like that. It was all treated, fumigated, flower of sulphur, till you was satisfied.'

The gardeners' working day was from 6 o'clock in the morning until 5 o'clock in Summer and from 7 o'clock until 4 o'clock in the Winter months, with half an hour for breakfast and an hour for lunch. Apart from greenhouse work their other duties included clearing leaves, digging borders, planting, mowing and watering the lawns although cutting the main lawn in front of the Hall was one of the Estate woodmen's tasks. The gravel drives had also to be kept free of weeds. Jobs such as scrubbing the greenhouses with insecticide or scraping vines were left for periods of bad weather.

Alterations to the gardens were made after the Hall was extended in 1906. These included a small formal garden to the east of the House and geranium beds and a sunken garden on the south side. The member of the family most keenly interested in their upkeep was Lady Sheffield and the work of the head gardeners was carefully scrutinised. As one remembers,

'If I knew what the Lady of the House wanted, I knew that was the main thing. If you kept her quiet you was all right.'

A feature of the Park, before it was demolished by the Army during the Second World War, was a little playhouse situated in the woods on the western 'wall side'.

'There used to be a cottage in the wood where the children used to go, cook their dinners, make toffee. There used to be a little stove there, boiler in one side for hot water and the oven in the other.'

It had bedrooms upstairs and a living room and it was played in by Sir Berkeley's daughter, Diana Sheffield and by his three sisters before her.

Another attraction in the Park was a model railway constructed in 1924 by Sir Berkeley Sheffield ostensibly for the purpose of training and interesting his sons in the mechanical side of railway operation. It was described in an article about Normanby Hall in the 'Hull Times' of November 17th, 1927:

'The metals or lines are laid on model sleepers, which run through cuttings, on the level and over embankments. It is complete with turntable,
engine shed, water tank, points worked by levers, in fact everything necessary to make the whole system a complete model railway. The three engines are perfect working models down to the smallest detail of those in use by the London and North Western, the Great Western and Great Northern Railways respectively, and are all capable of drawing with ease a human freight on their model trucks. It is amazing to find these Lilliputian steam engines, with their own heavy weight and with tender and trucks careering along their permanent way!'*

It was a source of great pleasure to the young son of the Sheffield family's head chauffeur,

'It made a big impression on me, I've still got a scar to this day where I came off one of the trucks! I was always fascinated by railways and I suppose at times when my father knew there was nobody around, or the family were all away, he would take me down there.'

One day his father,

'Pulled one of the locos out of the shed, and I spent a happy hour just polishing it with a dry duster you know, having the time of my life. I only ever saw it used once ... sneaking from behind the bushes; but on occasions, with my father's connivance, I would get one of those bogie things and run it down the track when nobody was in the Hall.'

By the 1930s, the miniature railway had fallen out of use when Sir Berkeley's children became adults. The track was eventually lifted and sold to a fairground operator in Mablethorpe. However the tradition of model railways in the Park is continued today by Scunthorpe Model Engineers.

Deer were also not new to Normanby when they were introduced to the Park in the large paddock behind the Hall in the 1960s. Traditionally, the sight of grazing deer in the grounds of a country house was a way of emphasising the noble ancestry of its owners. Three varieties had been reared there in a herd of some 200 animals and they were kept firmly at a distance by a stone built ha-ha or sunken wall, the remains of which can still be seen in the south of the Park. The head gamekeeper was in charge of looking after them and a cull was held annually in Autumn. After 1919 the deer were replaced by a prize herd of ferocious looking Highland cattle and later some 400 sheep from the Home Farm in Normanby Village.

The turntable and Sir Berkeley Sheffield's three replica model steam locomotives outside the engine house on 'Ice House Lane' also c.1930.

Sir Berkeley Sheffield inspecting two of his model steam locomotives in the Park c.1930.

The southern entrance to Normanby Park from 'Flixborough Corner' c.1910. In the caption of the original postcard 'Normanby' has unfortunately been wrongly spelt!

The original west entrance to the Hall opposite Normanby Village c.1930. It was replaced by far more elaborate iron gates and stone pillars later in the decade. On the left is the wicket gate which led to the 'servants' walk'.

The west range of the stableyard in a card postmarked the 11th of April 1919.

The main drive; Normanby Hall grounds looking west c.1900-1910. The servants' walk ran alongside this drive on the right.

Normanby Park Fire Brigade in full uniform in the stableyard in 1939. They are from the left, back; A. Ripley, T. Brown, R. Campbell, Barker (captain), Elliatt, T. Drayton. Front; J. Balderson, G. Carline, J. Armstrong, B. Slades, C. Gibbons. This photograph was taken after their abortive call out to a stack fire in Thealby, and the Brigade was disbanded soon afterwards.

Normanby Park fire engine in the stableyard c.1953, after its official retirement. The fireman is Joe Balderson.

Another photograph of the fire engine on the same day, when it was brought out of store as a children's attraction at a garden party held in the grounds of the Hall. With Joe Balderson the fireman, is Master Reginald Sheffield seated on the left.

Gwendoline Drive at around the turn of the 20th century. This ran north from the main drive to some gates on Thealby Lane, and was named after Sir Berkeley Sheffield's eldest sister.

View of the beautifully maintained grounds at Normanby c.1930. On the right is the east wall of the kitchen garden, and opposite are the tennis courts used by the family.

Gardeners at Normanby c.1910. Ernest Allen, the head gardener is seated in the centre wearing the straw hat, and behind him is Jane Langford who was in service at the Hall.

Inside the kitchen garden in the first decade of the 20th Century. Some of the large numbers of cut flowers grown for the Hall can be seen on the right.

Planting ornamental gardens at Normanby on July the 19th 1897. Standing on the right is the head gardener, Ernest Allen.

35

The lovely garden lake c.1930.

The children's playhouse in the woods on the western side of the Park c. 1900-1910.

SHOOTING AND THE NORMANBY ESTATE

In its heyday at around the turn of the century Normanby Hall was surrounded by a large estate consisting of approximately 10,000 acres. This stretched as far as Crosby to the south, West Halton to the north, Roxby to the east, and the River Trent to the west. Numerous farms worked this land, which were mainly leased out to tenant farmers, but the Sheffield family also employed a large number of estate workers. The Estate is mainly fertile arable land, especially the warp lands on the Trent side. There was little contact between the people who worked on the Estate and the House staff, and the former rarely visited the Hall.

The man responsible for the day-to-day running of the Estate was the estate agent .

'They always had somebody quite well-to-do. There was one called Corbett, there was Balfour, extremely nice fellow he was, there was Ponsonby, Atkinson-Clark. Atkinson-Clark's son, he followed him next. Then after the War things seemed to alter.'

The nerve centre of the Estate was the Estate Yard, or 'woodyard', which was situated just to the south of Normanby Village street. Between the Wars it was a bustling amalgam of workshops, stores and even an electricity generating station. The buildings still stand today but they have since been converted into houses. On the left of the entrance was the clerk of work's house who was in charge of the yard:

'As you went in through the gates, his house was on the left. Then there was a garage, then there was a little space round and then they started with Fred Richardson, his little office was the first one down that side. The second one was where bricklayers held their bit of stuff then there was a blacksmith's shop and then in the corner finishing that side coming towards the powerhouse was a joiner's shop. Then came the powerhouse and then next to that a plumber's and the old gentleman that ran the saw-mill.'

It attracted young boys growing up in the village like a magnet during school holidays, or even playtime from Normanby School. It was also where they would go to gather scraps of wood for the school stove.

'The workers would probably tolerate us for so long and kick us out. But it was fascinating because there was a blacksmith's shop in there, there was a saw-mill, there was a number of workshops where maintenance work was carried out for various parts of the Hall or the Estate. It was a ready-made playground for youngsters, I mean we used to enjoy ourselves in there.'

Sir Berkeley had a reputation for ensuring his property was kept in a state of good repair and the bulk of the Estate Yard's work consisted of maintenance and improvements to tenant farms, cottages and also to the Hall itself. Trees were felled on the estate when needed, then brought to the Estate Yard and cut up in a large saw-mill. There were also tanks for creosoting timber and any replacement doors, windows and roofing timbers were made in the yard. There was no full-time blacksmith, but Walter Goodhand came part-time from Flixborough.

A young apprentice joiner who started in the Estate Yard before the Second World War recalls:

'The sort of jobs we used to do was doors and windows for cottages, field gates, ten-foot field gates, small gates any sort of thing like that and work at the Hall. They got you into it straight away. And your wage was 10/- a week and we worked from 6 o'clock till 5 at night, half a crown a year rise and I'd got to 17/6d when I was called up.'

He also,

'Got a bit of cabinet-making as well. We repaired bits of furniture, quality furniture. Maybe put a new brass hinge on something, things like that, or a clock door that had gone.'

The various tradesmen cycled out to jobs and, although the foreman joiner owned a motorcycle (the only one in Normanby Village), he never used it at work. There was also a separate joiner's workshop in the Hall in the cellars beneath the servants' wing. A change to their usual routine came about in the shooting season when most of the workers in the Estate Yard were expected to act as beaters.

The most prominent building in the yard was the turbine-house or 'clock house', which generated electricity for the Hall but not for the Estate cottages in Normanby Village. Built in 1901, it can still be identified by its lantern tower and clock in the gable end, and it contained two large turbines, a generator and storage batteries.

With the coming of the Second World War, things changed dramatically however. Several of the estate-workers were called up and others transferred to John Sheffield's construction company at Conesby House.

This had been established by Sir Berkeley Sheffield's youngest son and when the War ended it took over all the repair and building work on the Estate. The Estate Yard thus became less important and a pale shadow of its former self.

After the War a firm called Marshall's took over part of the yard to renovate ex-Army trucks but the blacksmith's shop and the saw-mill still remained in use, the latter rented out as a private business. In addition the Estate woodmen still used the yard as their operating base. In later years it became completely derelict until it was resurrected as the housing estate of today.

Shooting has been a constant feature of life on the Normanby Estate and together with the neighbouring Appleby, Elsham, Manley, Scawby and Walcot Estates it has always enjoyed the reputation of being a top quality shooting property. It is well wooded and ideal for pheasants and partridges. However, fox hunting has never been a Normanby tradition.

Guests at family shoots often included well connected people as illustrated by the following report which appeared in a local newspaper at the end of the 19th century:

'A large shooting party has been entertained by

Sir Berkeley Sheffield at Normanby Park this week. Among the guests were H.R.H. the Duke of Cambridge, Colonel FitzGeorge, Lord and Lady Arthur Grosvenor, Lady Middleton, Lady Decie, Countess Cairns, Miss Beresford, Hon. Mr. Curzon, Hon. Derick Keppel, Colonel St. Quinton, Mr. Ward Jackson, and Mr. and Mrs. Edward St. Quinton. The covers round Normanby were well stocked with game, and excellent sport was enjoyed.'

The Sheffields employed a head gamekeeper, three under keepers and apprentice gamekeepers to safeguard their sporting interests. They tended to lead independent lives on their 'beats' and often stayed with the family for many years. Matthew Grass, for example, was head gamekeeper for most of the first half of this century and lived at Burton Wood House, or 'Wood House', on the road between Flixborough and Burton. He is remembered as,

'A real kind old gentleman. If somebody was ill or anything he would make sure they had a dinner, you know. If he saw you go poaching he'd have you, but he was one of the old timers. He would walk every day round his feeding points, he knew everything that was going on.'

Matthew was a member of the remarkable 'Grass' dynasty of gamekeepers who, at the turn of the 19th century, numbered over a hundred on country estates throughout Britain. They were all descended from two French brothers who arrived in Britain in the 18th century. Matthew's brother Fred worked for Lord St. Oswald at Appleby Hall. Gamekeepers were often appointed by word of mouth but jobs were also advertised in magazines

like 'The Gamekeeper'.

Another gamekeeper who served the family for a long period of time was Walter Atkinson who received his deputation, signed by Sir Berkeley Sheffield, on June 6th, 1905 and worked for the family for the next 62 years.

Walter had married a housemaid who worked for Richard Coulthurst, a farmer at Normanby Grange, and for the rest of their lives they lived at South Lodge near Scunthorpe where they brought up their two sons and three daughters. South Lodge was a Sheffield family shooting lodge and smallholding built in 1815 lying in woodland to the north of Ferry Road. It was common for gamekeepers to live in what was then an isolated location, as they needed peace and quiet to rear their gamebirds. Walter Atkinson became something of a local folk hero and the surrounding land became known as 'Atkinson's' or 'Akky's Warren'.

'He was very involved with his work. He was dedicated to it, and I think he did a very good job. He never switched off from it. He'd go out at night in his 70s if he thought there was poachers or anything about.'

The lodge had no water or electricity, only a pump in the backyard and candles or gas mantles for lighting. A black-leaded range was used for cooking. However to his visiting grandchildren it seemed like a marvellous rural retreat. Shooting parties also came on occasions as one of his daughters, Beryl Atkinson has recalled:

'It was a big day when they had pheasant

shoots. *After a morning shoot they would lunch at South Lodge Cottage. The food was brought in hot containers along with two footmen for serving the meals. After they had wined and dined we were invited to go and enjoy what was left and it was lovely being served by footmen. The smell of cigars and the taste of cooked birds was great. It was a big day for my father as the number of birds that were shot reflected on how good the rearing season had been.'*

Apart from rearing birds in the Summer, the gamekeepers' other duties were trapping vermin throughout the year, organising shooting parties and keeping a lookout for poachers. In the early years poaching was smaller in scale and not regarded as the serious offence it was later to become.

Shooting parties at Normanby before the Second World War were primarily for members of the family and their guests and they were held less frequently than they are today. Pheasant shooting began in late October and lasted until January. Partridges began a month earlier. Transport was mainly on foot and by bicycle except for horse and traps for the guns and a well turned out game cart with horse brasses brightly polished. Far more local children were employed as beaters in those days.

'They used to get different farmers and some of their friends, they'd come and stop at Normanby Hall, and they'd maybe have two or three days, and then maybe the farm labourers, somebody off the Estate would do the beating or gun-carrying. Well, they'd go to a certain area, they'd all meet up there. 'Course in them days it was horse-drawn

more than other vehicles. The gun-men knew where the beaters were so there was no accidents. And they'd sticks, and shout and bang you know, maybe going through a wood or long grass, anything to get those pheasants or rabbits. 'Course then they came out to the gun-men, they used to shoot 'em. Then they used to have their dogs for picking up. And gun carriers, they used to carry a spare gun. As they were shooting one off, the carrier was putting cartridges in the next and handing it over.'*

Another experienced beater recalls,

'They used to shoot Mondays, Fridays and Saturdays, and they used to go round Coleby on a Monday, and they used to go round Normanby and all that on the Friday, and do Burton Wood and all Flixborough on the Saturday. You see it was all routine, but then they only used to do it once a month.'

After four drives in the morning lunch was taken at midday at either a shooting lodge or a tenant farm followed by three drives in the afternoon. It was also hard work for the kitchen staff on shooting days:

'We used to have to pack their lunch up. They used to have shooting boxes, they were proper containers. The footmen used to go out and set their lunch up somewhere, in somebody's home or a gamekeeper's house. They used to have the same lunch out, and beaters, we used to make large stews of this venison you know and put some baked potatoes on the top. Even the beaters had a good hot meal.'

Nevertheless beating could occasionally be dangerous , as a young under keeper in the 1950s recalls:

'I can remember Joe Balderson used to be a flanker and I remember down Bullwell, Joe was just coming up one side with the old flag and somebody shot, blew a hole in the flag! And old Joe was mad when he came up there, he didn't half lay into this chap.'

At the end of the shoot the gamekeepers returned to Normanby and unloaded the pheasants, hares and even woodcock from the game cart into the game larder. After tea this was where the results of the day's shoot were sorted and graded. Any surplus was sold to a butcher's in Scunthorpe but a fair proportion was saved for the Hall. Tips received by the gamekeepers were shared out evenly by the head gamekeeper.

In addition to their salary they also,

'Used to get a suit of clothes, I think it was every two years. That was found for them and eventually they just bought them a Tweed jacket, waistcoat and a cap.'

In earlier years the gamekeepers wore a special uniform on shooting days, complete with a stove-pipe hat and brass buttons marked with 'BS', for Berkeley Sheffield. However, they were extremely uncomfortable and heartily disliked!

The highlight of the year on the Normanby Estate was undoubtedly the annual Normanby Park Show organised by Normanby Estates Agricultural and Horticultural Society and held in the grounds of the Hall. The first Show was in 1884 and despite the agricultural depression of the time it flourished until the outbreak of the First World War. It was never successfully revived after 1914 however and the story goes that the band and a detachment of soldiers from the Royal Scots Greys who were performing at the Show were actually mobilised on the day of the last Show!

In the early years of this century it had become a day long event with the horticultural show starting on the preceding evening. The show, which attracted visitors and competitors from far and wide, all dressed in their 'Sunday best'. Remains of the 'half moon' public entrance to the Show can still be seen in the western perimeter wall of the Park, between the Main and South gates:

'It was marvellous, there used to be all these tents and a Guards' band used to come and play and there used to be fireworks at night. That was the thing of the year, the only place for us to go you see when I was a child.'

In 1913, the day began at 10.00 a.m. and apart from inspecting the numerous marquees containing agricultural horses, cattle, fruit, pigs, poultry, produce, sheep and vegetables, visitors could also enjoy the lovely grounds of the Park and extensive greenhouses. Music was provided by two military bands and a bandstand was set up on the main lawn outside the Hall.

'My mother and my grandfather used to walk from Crosby to the Show, and they had a splendid band, and I've heard them say that my grandfather he was sat jiffling his feet about to the music all day.'

At 1.00 p.m., a public lunch presided over by Sir Berkeley was held costing 2/6d. There were also sporting events, although they seem to have been discontinued in the final years. In 1905 they included 'one mile bicycle handicap races' on penny farthing bicycles and Edwardian novelty contests such as 'potato races (mounted)', 'ladies arithmetic races', 'apple race' and 'egg and ladle races (mounted)'. Instructions for the latter were printed in the programme as follows,

'Competitors to ride a point, dismount, pick up egg with ladle, gallop round a post and back to winning post. If an egg is dropped, competitors must dismount and pick it up again.'

The more serious show competitions were organised in three sections: agricultural horses and livestock, poultry, and produce and horticulture. The many classes were broadly divided into local ones open to tenants of the Normanby Estate and open classes for all comers. All were fiercely contested. There was also a separate children's class for the best display of a bouquet of wild flowers for which the princely sum of 5/- was awarded to each of the winners in the three age categories.

However, winning a prize could have its drawbacks:

'My father won first prize for cottage pig at one of them. I'll tell you how hard up the doctors were in those days. Old Doctor Baker called to see my mother and he says, 'Oh I hear George won first prize for the pig at the Show'. So my mother says, 'Yes you'd better have it'. And she paid the doctor's bill with it.'

Exhibits in the horticultural section of the Show were traditionally judged by head gardeners from other country houses and the head gardener at Normanby in the late 1930s regularly judged at nearby shows. Sometimes small glasses of whisky were 'accidentally' left beside exhibits as an inducement! However, growing for purely showing purposes was not encouraged in the kitchen gardens at Normanby, as he remembers:

'Lady Sheffield says, 'I don't mind you showing but I don't want any of your show stuff, I want young stuff. I mean you waste such a lot of vegetables on things like that. No, you're inclined to neglect your other work if you're going in for showing.'

Normanby Show was particularly exciting for children as one woman who visited it as a girl remembers:

'To us kiddies it was a day we always remembered. It was made happy for us kids.'

But all good things have to come to an end, and the day was concluded with an elaborate display of fireworks and a rendition of 'God Save the King'. Special late trains then ran from Frodingham station to Grimsby and to Barnsley and intermediate stations but a more leisurely return home to Gainsborough, Goole and Hull could be had by excursion steamboats which left earlier in the evening from Burton Stather.

Ring Fence Map produced for Sir Berkeley Sheffield in 1898 showing the extent of the Normanby Estate surrounding Normanby Hall.

Inside Normanby Estate Yard in 1907, with an array of build
material in the centre neatly arranged for the photographer.

The Normanby Estate staff taken in the Estateyard after
snowfall around 1926. There are no less than 52 people her
and it is thought to be the leaving photograph of the estate age
Mr. Gilbert Balfour. He is seated on the front row holding t
puppy.

Interior of the machine shop, Normanby Estate Yard.

A view of the immaculately maintained interior of the 'clock house' in Normanby Estate Yard in 1907. It shows the generating equipment which produced electricity for the Hall.

A two horse cart inside Normanby Estateyard, c.1920.

A shire horse from the Normanby Park Stud. Sir Berkeley Sheffield had a stud of shire horses in Normanby Village during the first decades of the 20th Century. They were paraded at some of the last Normanby Park Shows.

The scene after a 'top rabbit shoot' on the Normanby Estate c.1950. Standing in the centre are two of the Estate gamekeepers; Walter Atkinson wearing his distinctive trilby hat on the left alongside Jack Dent. Kneeling are Walter's two sons, Doug on the left and Harry on the right. 'Top rabbit shoots' were occasions when gamekeepers and their friends were allowed to shoot on the Estate for sport.

Walter Atkinson on the front at Cleethorpes on August the 26th 1951. This is thought to have been his only ever visit to the resort.

Eva Thompson the youngest of gamekeeper Walter Atkinson's three daughters outside South Lodge, Atkinson's Warren in the 1950's. This was the Sheffield family shooting lodge closest to Scunthorpe, and it was where Walter Atkinson lived and farmed for many years after 1905.

Walter Atkinson leading a horse carrying the eldest and youngest of his three daughters; 'Bobs' in front and Eva behind her. The gentleman on the right is possibly Bill Leaning.

Photograph taken after a shooting party on the Normanby Estate. It consists of gamekeepers and their friends and relatives.

A scene in a stackyard during shooting on the Normanby Estate in 1927. In the centre holding the pheasants is Walter Atkinson, and another Sheffield family gamekeeper, Matthew Grass is standing second from the left.

SLIPTON KING, S.H.S.B. 26692.

NORMANBY PARK.

THURSDAY, JULY 27th, 1911.

The front cover of a Normanby Show catalogue and programme held on July 27th 1911.

The main arena, Normanby Park Show, taken from an upper storey window in the Hall at some point between 1906 and 1914. An interesting aspect of this photograph is the temporary walkway on the right which allowed spectators to cross the ha-ha into the Deer Park.

Crowd scenes in the stands surrounding the main arena at the Normanby Park Show held on the 25th of July 1907. The baby held between the gap in the railings, is thought to be Sir Berkeley Sheffield's eldest son, Robert.

A lovely Edwardian photograph of one of the Shows held around 1910. The well-dressed audience is listening to a band on the main lawn outside the Hall.

Normanby Estates Agricultural & Horticultural Society Show Committee in the early years of the 20th Century. Amongst those standing on the back row are Ernest Dain, James Sutton, Billy Wood, Arthur Rowbottom and Godfrey Gillatt.

Horticultural displays at the Show of 1907.

A 'penny farthing' bicycle race at Normanby Park Show in 1908. By this time 'penny farthing' bicycles had become obsolete, so the races would have been something of a novelty attraction.

Catalogue of an auction sale held in 1919 of part of the Normanby Estate between Scunthorpe and Gunness.

A YEAR IN THE LIFE

Between the Wars, a year in the life of the household adhered to a strict seasonal timetable which rarely altered. After Winter at Normanby a house was rented at Newmarket in March for the start of the flat racing season. This was followed by a week spent in London and then back to Newmarket for a further week's racing. The Summer months were filled with a round of dinners, race meetings, Royal garden fetes and social calls collectively known as the 'London Season'. Then Autumn and the beginning of the grouse shooting season. The family then travelled to Meoble Forest on the west coast of Scotland, before finally returning to Normanby in October.

Visiting Normanby today, it is difficult to envisage that the family resided here for only five months of every year. Moreover, Sir Berkeley spent even more time in London during his periods of office as the Member of Parliament for the local North Lindsey (Brigg) Parliamentary Division. It was a way of life that attempted to balance the activities of living in town and country on one hand with those of responsibility and pleasure.

Many of the Normanby house staff travelled down to London with the family and they included the cook, first kitchen-maid, scullery-maid, two footmen and one of the housemaids. The second kitchen-maid, however, remained at Normanby jam-making with the housekeeper. They made enough jam and marmalade for an entire year in the still-room and this was the only time it was used for the purpose it had been designed for.

Strawberry jam was a particular favourite! The remaining staff also had to completely spring-clean the Hall and it was often re-painted. Heavy carpets were taken out on to the main lawn and beaten with sticks before being dragged over the grass to freshen them up. The head chauffeur moved to London motoring down separately with the various cars in a relay operation. His duties there entailed far more driving during the Summer months than at Normanby.

In the early years of this Century, the family's residence was an imposing Victorian house at 8 South Audley Street close to Hyde Park.

'South Audley Street was a huge house, it was eight storeys high, and down in the basement there were two horses and carts. Wagons could pass in the basement.'

However, it was sold in 1922, and the family lived in rented houses before purchasing 16 Kensington Palace Gardens on the western fringe of Hyde Park.

'Number 16 Kensington Palace Gardens, I'll never forget that one. That was actually a private road that ran between Notting Hill Gate and High Street Kensington. There were huge wrought iron gates with gilt-edged trimmings at either end of the road, gate-masters with long green coats and top hats, and the road was completely barred other than to residents or necessary vehicles ... it was a large obviously stately house; Kensington Palace Gardens was a whole row of these very luxurious mansions. It contained a number of embassies, the Russsian Embassy was almost opposite Number 16, the Turkish Embassy or one of the eastern

embassies just a little bit further up, and all obviously belonging to the really upper classes; no-one could afford them even in those days. It was a very impressive looking building from the front.'

Today, Kensington Palace Gardens is still a private road, and retains the wealthy appearance of a 'Victorian millionaires' row'.

For the domestic staff, a spell in London with the family was an exciting prospect and a welcome change from their usual routine. Their quarters were in the basement but the chauffeur and his family had a separate flat above the garages. Summer food such as chicken, lamb and salmon featured on the menu and produce was sent down from the kitchen garden at Normanby. The house had a happy atmosphere enjoyed by both the family and staff.

On a typical day off the servants would,

'Go into Hyde Park, we used to go down to Selfridges and look round the shops; you came out at Oxford Street and we'd look round there. We'd have our tea in a Lyon's Corner House for a shilling I think it would be, then on to either a play or pictures. Now you're saying, how could we afford that on 28 pounds a year ? But you see, we didn't have any food to pay for, we only had our clothes and pleasure and things were cheap.'

In August, the family and accompanying retinue left London and travelled to Meoble Forest on the west coast of Scotland. There they owned an estate and shooting lodge in the idyllic setting of Loch Morar, a few miles east of Mallaig. Loch Morar is the deepest loch in Scotland and is even rumoured to have its own monster!

They went by train from Scunthorpe and Frodingham station, after a few days spent preparing for the journey at Normanby. A private coach with sleeping accommodation was attached to scheduled trains between Doncaster and Morar, the last stop before Mallaig on the West Highland line. The final leg of the journey was across the 12 mile length of Loch Morar by motor launch. Supper and breakfast for the trip were prepared in hampers by the kitchen staff beforehand.

'We never had to change. Well we took such a lot with us you know. We used to get there about just after lunch next day, they used to travel all night. And we had sleepers. It was lovely that twelve mile on the water when you got there.'

Meoble Forest was a large shooting lodge, which for the domestic staff was,

'Free and easy you know. They used to go up on the hills, we used to pack them up, they used to go up on the hills shooting.'

On their Sunday days off the family's boatman would take them into Mallaig by barge, or they would simply picnic in the lovely Highland countryside. Venison shot at Meoble Forest was taken back to Normanby and served in the dining room. The lodge was used by the Army for training purposes during the Second World War and relinquished by the family soon afterwards.

Christmas at Normanby was a big family occasion and the time of year when the largest number of visitors were entertained at the Hall occurring as it does, in the middle of the shooting season. Shooting parties were the mainstay of social life at Normanby.

'Christmas time was out of this world. You used to make a hundred plum puddings but they were all the same recipe and then Lady Sheffield used to take them to the old people in Thealby and Normanby. We used to make a lot of little ones you know. Now they took some boiling a hundred plum puddings. Then we used to have four turkeys on Christmas Day, we always used to have a house full at Christmas.'

Later, in the 1950s, Christmas parties were held for all the children of the estate staff in the two drawing rooms in the Hall.

A frequent visitor in the early years was the second eldest of Sir Berkeley Sheffield's three sisters, Lady Arthur Grosvenor, who was wont to arrive in a pair of gypsy caravans, a somewhat odd means of transport for the wife of one of the richest men in England!

'I think I would be seven or eight and we were walking along that Thealby Road, then there was this woman coming with this huge dog. I was terrified. She asked us over to her caravan. It was marvellous and she'd another couple with her, they'd a caravan on their own. And she'd a lovely blue frock on right to the ground with silver braid. And this huge dog, it was as big as me. She said, 'It won't hurt you, won't hurt you.' Nearly knocked me down.'

There were also, of course, a number of famous visitors to the Hall including, in the 1930s, H.R.H. Prince George when he came to Scunthorpe in October 1933 to open the Scunthorpe Section of the Doncaster-Grimsby trunk road (now known as Kingsway and Queensway). He planted a tulip tree in the grounds to commemorate his stay.

The Man and the Family North Lindsey
delights to honour.

Sir Berkeley Sheffield with his wife and three of their children taken in the main entrance of the Hall. The photograph was used in publicity material during the general election of 1910, when he stood as a Unionist candidate in the local North Lindsey (Brigg) Parliamentary Division.

Lady Julia Sheffield holding her youngest son John, and surrounded by the rest of her children on the steps of the Hall during the First World War. They are clockwise from the left, Robert, Reginald, George and Diana. Two of the boys are dressed in military uniform.

Sir Berkeley Sheffield's first motorcar taken at Normanby after the turn of the 20th Century. He is not in this photograph however.

Meoble Forest, close to Loch Morar on the West Coast of Scotland, c.1927-32. This was a Sheffield family shooting lodge and holiday home.

Sheffield family staff picnic at Loch Morar, c.1927-32. They are from the left; a housemaid, a boatman, Lilly Marshall (scullerymaid), 'Charles' (the Head footman), and another housemaid. The housemaid on the left was a Scots girl and not from Normanby.

Burton Stather bell ringers seated on the steps of the main staircase at the Hall in 1923. They used to play a special Christmas programme of carols and some change ringing at Normanby and also at St. Andrew's church in Burton.

Lady Arthur Grosvenor's gypsy caravans in the grounds of the Park after the turn of the 20th Century.

Hand written luncheon menu for the visit of H.R.H. Prince George on October the 26th 1933.

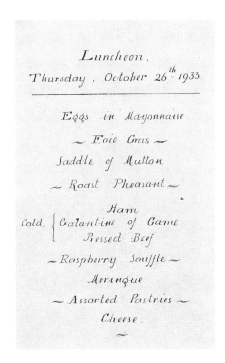

Luncheon.

Thursday, October 26th 1933.

Eggs in Mayonnaise

~ Foie Gras ~

Saddle of Mutton

~ Roast Pheasant ~

Cold. { Ham
Galantine of Game
Pressed Beef

~ Raspberry Souffle ~

Meringue

~ Assorted Pastries ~

Cheese.

~

Children's Christmas party at Normanby Hall in front of the main staircase during the 1950's. Helping Santa in the centre is Mrs Nancy Sheffield, and behind her the Vicar of Burton and his wife.

WAR YEARS

During the First World War, Normanby Hall, like other similar country houses in Britain, became a Voluntary Aid Detachment Hospital for convalescing soldiers through the generosity of Sir Berkeley Sheffield. A young girl who started work at the Hall during that period remembers,

'It was a hospital when I went for the soldiers. They all came from Sheffield you see and they used to come backwards and forwards. Some of them were quite ill when they came, and some of them were just recuperating ... there was a matron there and lots of V.A.D. nurses and Lady Sheffield was the Commandant. She wore a different uniform to all the others. They just kept one wing for themselves, Sir Berkeley's study was turned into a dining room, and that's really the only room they had downstairs. The soldiers had all the downstairs.'

Several of the rooms on the ground floor were converted into wards to treat the 60 or so soldiers that occupied the Hall. The nursing staff consisted of a trained sister and a matron as well as volunteer nurses from the nearby villages. One was Clara Spilman, who later became a governess and travelled widely in Europe, Egypt and Abyssinia. She is thought to have been the first English-woman to visit the Ethiopian capital of Addis Ababa. Lady Julia Sheffield was the Commandant in overall charge and she received several honours for her exemplary work, including twice being mentioned in despatches.

A newcomer to the area was Mr Miranda from India, who had commenced studies in England when the War broke out.

'He came to Normanby voluntarily to drive the cars you see. He used to drive the soldiers about in what we used to call the 'Silent Night'. It was a big Daimler, and he used to fetch them from Sheffield and take them back again. Then he would take them to the pictures and all that sort of thing. He didn't get any wages and came into the servants' hall for his meals. He was a gentleman.'

The recuperating soldiers wore the traditional blue uniforms and could often be seen relaxing in the grounds of the Hall. They proved to be something of an attraction to at least one young lady growing up in the area, much to the chagrin of her parents when they found out!

Sir Berkeley Sheffield had a distinguished career as a Staff Officer and diplomat during the War, which took him away from Normanby for much of the period. He was, for example, Acting Private Secretary to Viscount Milner with the Allied Mission in Petrograd, Russia for which he was awarded the Order of St. Anne (3rd Class). His children meanwhile were either away at boarding school or occupied rooms on the top floor of the Hall, including a nursery and a schoolroom. They were looked after by a French governess, a schoolroom-maid, a nanny, under-nanny and a nursery-maid.

On Armistice Day, a fancy dress party was held to celebrate the great event in the dining room and the beds were pushed to one side. All the soldiers had left by January 1919 and the Hall soon reverted back to being a family home. The staff, including the returning butler and footmen, then had the laborious task of restoring it to its pre-War condition.

After the War had ended Sir Berkeley employed his former batman as a valet, a practice that was quite common at the time.

'There used to be his valet, he'd been wounded in the War, he walked on crutches, but Sir Berkeley had him living there again you see, and he used to bring his clothes and I used to carry them upstairs for him and then he used to go up in the lift and put them away. He used to sit and clean the silver and I used to carry it to the dining room and he would hop along on his crutches and set the table you see. He was a great help really.'

Today, the only reminder of the use of the Hall as a hospital is a framed commemorative certificate hanging in the entrance hall, but a Flixborough man who came to work at Normanby as a farm foreman in 1962 recalls that one of his first jobs was to clear out the old Estateyard.

'I remember on top of the beams in the old joiner's shop, was a kind of board and we looked at it closely, it had letters fetched out of it, and it spelt 'Welcome Home'. It was from the end of the First World War and it'd be lit up by some kind of light behind it and show 'Welcome Home' to people returning from the First World War. It was still there at the top of the joiner's shop.'

When hostilities reopened in 1939, Normanby was once again pressed into service as one of many country houses requisitioned by the armed forces under the Compensation Defence Act of 1939. Thus, in June 1940, the Hall became a military headquarters and the Sheffield family moved into the large house in Normanby Village known locally as 'Little Normanby'. The house was redecorated and an air raid shelter assembled in the library.

'Little Normanby' was at the centre of the Home Farm, which had been built by the Sheffield family as a model farm in the late 19th century and at the outbreak of war was tenanted by a farmer called George Sheardown. Although a large residence in its own right, with some 12 bedrooms, it is considerably smaller than the Hall. The family were thus joined by a much reduced staff, consisting of the butler Mr Cooper, the cook Mrs McKenzie, the head housemaid, a kitchen-maid and another housemaid. The head chauffeur and his family continued to live in the Park however, although the cars were garaged at 'Little Normanby'. A housemaid who worked at 'Little Normanby' recalls that a frequent visitor was Lady Portman:

'Sir Berkeley's sister, Lady Portman, used to come from Healing Manor. She had a parrot, it was a thing. She used to put a sheet out and stand this parrot on this stand and it used to shout. I didn't like the thing, it used to throw nuts and things.'

Soon after the outbreak of War an air raid shelter was added to the rear of the Hall leading into the cellars beneath the servants' quarters. It had heavy iron doors at each end, and was lined with beds. In the event of bomb damage, it would have acted as an escape route into the Park. The shelter is still in existence today, and for many years was used as a service entrance into the cellars.

Before the military arrived extensive preparations were made at the Hall. A young estate joiner who joined the Fleet Air Arm the following year remembers that,

'1940 was when the Army took over and that's when we took everything up. Some furniture we took to Doncaster and stored with a professional storage thing but we did store a lot of stuff in the two drawing rooms. All the carpets and all the furniture that didn't go away was all stored in those two rooms. When the soldiers came in the cellars were full of wines, spirits and everything, and to make it extra safe, that wooden door, we screwed convex steel in to stop 'em chopping through with axes, to keep 'em out! By gosh there was some stuff there. All their wines and spirits and such like from London was brought and put in with their stock at this end. I remember cleaning it out, and there was hundreds and hundreds of bottles.'

In the final month before the Army arrived the Hall was left empty, and Joe Balderson an estate bricklayer and general craftsman, was asked to sleep there. His daughter remembers:

'I know my dad went for two or three nights and it was a bit lonely so my mother and I went with him and we slept there, just the three of us in this huge building and I don't know, perhaps a month until the military came in.'

During that time, the only serious bombing incident occurred on May 12th, 1940, when the former Nitrogen Fertilisers works at Flixborough was hit, killing five men and injuring six more. However local residents well remember Hull being bombed when it was possible to read at night by the light of the burning city in Normanby Village.

'We could see Hull being bombed, we could see the fire, you know the sky would be lit up. You'd think, 'Oh Hull's got it again'.'

The first troops to occupy the Hall in June 1940 were Royal Artillery anti-aircraft units who manned the various Ack-Ack batteries sent to Scunthorpe to counter expected air attacks. One unit arriving in December 1941 was greatly impressed by the welcoming crowds in Oswald Road and Frodingham Road, only realising later they had gathered to watch a 'Warship Week' parade! The garage block in the stableyard was used as the main storage point for their rations and a lorry went out on a daily basis to supply each gunsite.

In April 1944, before 'D' Day, the surrounding fields, woodland and the Park were suddenly taken over by large numbers of Canadian troops involved in a training exercise on the River Trent. The exercise, codenamed 'Kate', was intended as practice for units of the 2nd Canadian Infantry Division for crossing a tidal estuary, in this case, the River Seine in France. A former Thealby resident remembers:

'When the Canadians first came in it was real hot summery weather and they stopped in that little three-cornered pinfold as we called it outside my mother's house in Thealby. They used to run a little shop, sweets and tobacco and such like, and of course they used to give them lemonade and

whatever. One of the officers went to her when he found out, 'You can't afford to do that'. 'Look' she said, 'They're a long way from home, I've two lads a long way from home, I hope somebody'll do the same for them'. Anyway, she never lost by it, they used to see she was all right if there was a little bit of black-marketeering passing that way !'

However, the most important military activity at Normanby Hall during the War and, indeed, in the Scunthorpe area as a whole, was undertaken by 'B' Squadron, Assault Wing, of the Assault Training and Development Centre. Based at Gosport in Hampshire they were themselves an offshoot of the Specialised Armour Development Establishment and originally moved to the Normanby area in late 1944 to train a Regiment on the Trent for crossing the Rhine. The Trent at Burton was chosen, because it exactly duplicated the current, speed of tide and width of the German river. This plan was overtaken by the course of events however, but the unit stayed on in the area experimenting with amphibious armoured vehicles.

The troops were mainly billeted in the bedrooms in the former servants' quarters, with the courtyard at the north acting as their parade ground. The kitchen was the cookhouse and the servants' hall their messroom. Laundry was sent to Grimsby by lorry and some Italian Prisoners of War were even brought in to do fatigues and cookhouse duties. They were regarded as ideal quarters and, like many servicemen of their generation, they briefly enjoyed the experience of living in a country house. One tank man who had joined the Army in 1936 remembers that, in the closing months of the War:

'There weren't many of us in one room and when you looked out of the windows you were in a comfortable place. It was maybe cold outside and to see the trees there after being abroad in the Middle East and have a place like that. I mean it was a little bit of home life, or semi-home life again.'

Social life for the unit consisted of a walk up to the Sheffield Arms in Burton, weekly dances in the Village Hall which was also used as a Wartime canteen, or an evening trip to Scunthorpe in the 'liberty truck'. This was parked on Market Hill, and returned to the Hall after closing time. There were also occasional dances in the Hall itself such as a 'Thankyou party' for all the local people who had acted as hosts to members of the squadron and to which office girls from Lysaght's Works were invited. One Captain in the unit used his free time more contructively however. He made furniture in the the workshop in the cellars of the Hall in readiness for setting up home after his forthcoming marriage.

The dances in the Village Hall at Burton were usually held on Tuesdays. They were popular not just with villagers and the troops based at the Hall but also with girls from Scunthorpe who were either walked home or taken back by Army lorry in the small hours of the morning. The V.E. (Victory in Europe) night dance was particularly memorable for one Corporal because,

'I didn't dance a great lot, I'd only got the rudiments, but I thought seeing it was V.E. night I thought I might as well go and have a look and I got my courage up by going into the Sheffield Arms. I thought this is it I'll go, and that's how I

met my wife, my future sweetheart.'

Civilian life in Normanby Village changed quite a lot during the War years. The Estate Yard was run down, but it was never used for military purposes. Perhaps surprisingly for such a small place, there was a Home Guard unit in Normanby as well as Air Raid Precautions. The village schoolmaster Thomas Sumpter was in charge of the latter and their headquarters were in Normanby School. It was here that in 1939 domestic staff from the Hall went to fetch their gasmasks.

'Well the A.R.P. really was a group of more elderly people who were too old to serve in the forces and they did their best by being trained for fire-fighting and for observing and helping first aid in case of bomb attack. They had to make sure everybody kept their windows blacked out in accordance with regulations. No lights were allowed to show from houses, so they were responsible for going round the village.'

Thomas Sumpter's son also remembers that the only serious incident in which they were involved,

'Was a suspicion that some large explosive bombs had been dropped in a large field just adjoining the rear entrance to the Hall grounds. I remember father being called out, various people inspecting it and they decided that there was nothing there, just the crater and that was it. My father wasn't very happy about this and about two months later he got the bomb disposal people out and discovered there was an unexploded bomb about twenty feet down and it had to be excavated.'

Similarly the Normanby Home Guard was mostly made up of estate workers, commanded by 2nd Lt. Frank Heritage, the Sheffield family's head chauffeur. They had,

'All the usual lectures, drill sessions. They used to patrol the village, they used to post sentries throughout the village and the area surrounding the Park 24 hours a day. There was always at least one Home Guard carrying a rifle somewhere on the Normanby Road.'

The Hall was eventually closed as a Water Assault base on December 31st, 1945, and the last remaining personnel were transferred back to Gosport. It was in relatively good condition when it was finally returned back to its owners, although the Park, apart from the kitchen garden, had become overgrown during the Army's occupation.

Group of patients and nursing staff on the steps of the Hall during the First World War.

Soldiers behind the main Hall after it had been converted into a hospital.

Recuperating servicemen, mostly in fancy dress, taken outside the garden entrance during the First World War.

Inside the Hall in the Great War, showing soldiers and the matron. The photograph was taken in the dining room, the largest of the downstairs rooms to be turned into a ward.

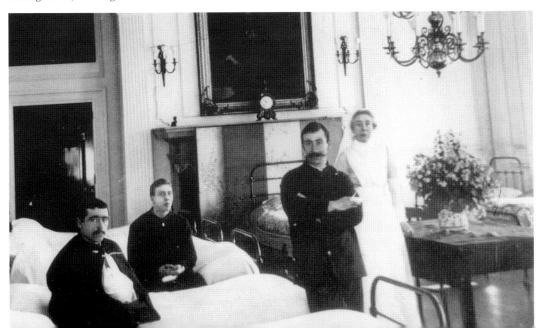

Group of nurses in the grounds of the Hall. Seated second from the right is the matron.

Sergeants' mess dinner at the Hall in 1943.

An amphibious tank used in the trials conducted by the Water Assault Unit. Burton Hills can be seen in the background. (Photograph courtesy of the Tank Museum).

The concrete slipway at Burton Stather constructed for the Water Assault Unit, with an amphibious tank waiting to enter the river. (Photograph courtesy of the Tank Museum).

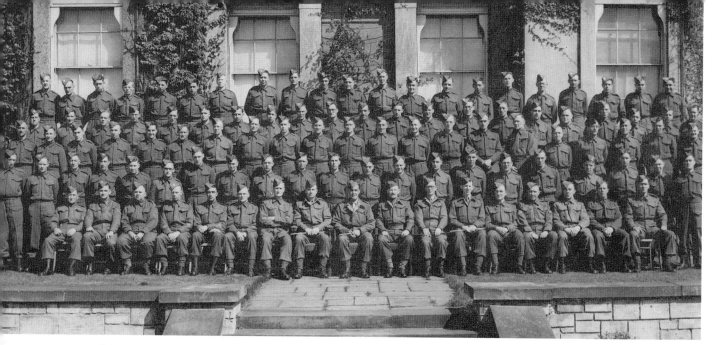

One of the first Army units based at the Hall during the Second World War was the 926 (H.A.A.) Home Ack Ack unit, shown here on the south side of the Hall.

Frank Drayton on the left and Joe Balderson on the right of Normanby Home Guard taken outside one of the houses in Normanby Village.

Military personnel of 'B' Squadron, Water Assault Wing of the Assault Training and Development Centre, taken outside the Hall in 1945.

The full line up is;

Back row; Private Hardy. Craftsmen Galloway, Hemp, Rayner, Ellis, Normington, Montgomery, Rudnitsky, Nash.
Third row; Privates Critchley, Bradley. Troopers Stanford, Clark, Buchanan, Porteous, Humphreys, Nelson, Bee, Bogue, Horley, Hopkinson.
Second row; Troopers Wilkinson, Wibberley, Vincent, Gibb, Moult, Walters, Pollard, Sayer, Kane, Coles, Lilley, Smith, Stewart, Haigh.
Front row; Lance Corporal Jackson. Corporals Holmes, Mundle. Sergeants Roberts, Fulcher, Baillie, Newton. Squadron Quarter Master Sergeant May. Major G.R. Heyland M.C., Captain B.C. Marsh, Squadron Sergeant Major Glanville, Staff Sergeant Woodcock, Sergeants Luckhurst, Bott, Geddes.Corporals George, Pellegrinetti.

Amphibious tank about to reach the foreshore at Burton Stather after crossing the Trent. (Photograph courtesy of the Tank Museum).

Two mechanics from the Water Assault Unit; David Gibb on the left with Gordon 'Darkie' Stone. They are standing in front of a makeshift canvas workshop down at the Stather, but some distance from the Trent side.

Normanby Home Guard.

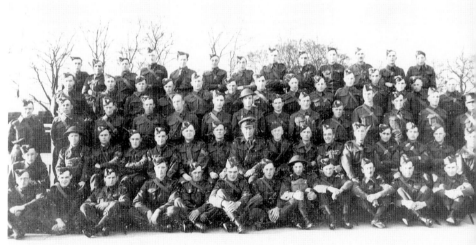

VILLAGE LIFE

Sheffield family influence has always been great in the four main villages close to Normanby Hall, which are Burton, Flixborough, Normanby and Thealby, and at one time most of the property was owned by them. Before the Second World War, all the 25 or so dwellings in Normanby Village were leased to estate workers or former estate workers to the extent that holders of individual jobs, such as the Normanby schoolmaster, always lived in the same house or cottage. Traditionally he resided next door to, and under the same roof as, the butler at the Hall. The cottages are older than the houses and, according to local legend, the family would at one time not allow the building of houses with upstairs windows, as this would allow their tenants to look down on them as they passed by in their carriages. Some still bear the traditional stamp of an estate property, the 'boar's head' crest of the Sheffield family.

Since the last War things have changed a great deal, although to the untutored eye Normanby still retains the appearance of a well kept estate village. Estate villages are something of a Lincolnshire speciality. One of the soldiers in the Water Assault Wing remembers,

'When I first saw it, it was absolutely beautiful and I always thought there must be some people with money living in those houses. I didn't realise they were estate workers who lived on the estate.'

The residents took great pride in the appearance of the village and the upkeep of their gardens, but nowadays very few people with Hall or Estate connections still live there. There were never a lot of facilities but at one time there was a post office opposite the Estate office and even a village school. This was a small brick building of just two classrooms, situated on the northern side of the village street a couple of doors along from the main gates of the Hall. A third wooden classroom was later added at the rear. The school was built in 1864, but closed on November 30th, 1939 with the opening of a new primary school in Burton Stather, and has now been demolished.

The schoolmaster until his retirement in 1930 was Mr Wilkes, (affectionately known as 'gaffer'), who was succeeded by Thomas Sumpter up to the school's final demise. It was then a boys' only primary school serving Burton, Flixborough, Normanby and Thealby but it had been a mixed school in the 19th century. In those days the schoolmaster was the only person in the village not directly employed by the Sheffield Family but he occupied his house rent free and had two assistant teachers. The school football pitch lay in a grass field on the left hand side of the Normanby road just before the left hand turn into the village and the school also had its own garden a few doors up. A former pupil remembers that:

'There was a little playground, it obviously wasn't big enough, so we were allowed to go anywhere at playtime. The boys who lived in Normanby could go home at playtime and we used to go into the field on the Scunthorpe road there and play cricket or football. Then when our time was up, old 'gaffer' Wilkes would walk out the school across the road, through the Estate Yard, and blow a whistle. Then we would wander round

by the road and back to school.'

At Christmas time,

'They had a free party in the schoolroom and there was a big Christmas tree and every schoolchild in the district came that night and then after a meal they used to call the names out and you'd go up and receive your present.'

Thomas Sumpter the last schoolmaster was,

'A very keen sportsman, very keen on his cricket and hockey, and he always had very successful football sides. He was also very keen on the Scunthorpe Music and Drama festival and his pupils regularly won prizes for singing and elocution. Otherwise it was a typical village school where the pupils were not very well off, but nevertheless were very happy. The children walked from Thealby, Flixborough and Burton through all weathers. The school was very basic, the toilet block being across the school playground, and the cloakroom a very small room.'

He was also,

'A good schoolmaster. I should say he was the finest schoolmaster there's ever been in Scunthorpe or the Scunthorpe area. He was good at everything, gardening, football, cricket, any sports.'

When Normanby School closed, Thomas Sumpter became the Headmaster of Brumby Secondary School in Scunthorpe, but continued to live in the village because he believed that with the War, it would be safer for his family. He later became Headmaster of Westcliff Secondary School which was renamed after him.

In the first decades of the 20th century, amenities were primitive to say the least in the villages surrounding the Hall, electricity only arriving at Normanby just before the Second World War. Some houses had to wait until the 1960s for proper sanitary facilities.

'None of the villages had a bathroom, you had to have a bath in front of the fire. We had a big zinc bath and you used to have to boil the water and carry it in buckets to your bath. Same on wash days, you had to light the copper. We used to go in the woods collecting sticks to light the copper with. All hard work in those days.'

Most of the villagers had vegetable gardens and fruit trees, but bread, fish, meat and provisions were delivered to the door. They also kept chickens and a pig,

'Cottages used to have their own pig, and we used to have a glut when it was first killed. But what we used to do, you all killed your pigs at a different time and everyone used to send about half a dozen frys out to different people you know, a bit of liver, a bit of kidney meat and all your relatives got a pork pie and sausage and all that sort of thing. And then of course my father used to salt all the hams and his flitches as they called it and shoulders. And then you used to have your ham and that for the year more or less.'

Social life in Normanby Village mainly revolved around Normanby Cricket Club, with its idyllic ground surrounded by seating at the southern end of the Park .

'On Saturday I know my mother would take us down as children and no doubt I spent my childhood there on a Saturday. A Mrs Gray from Thealby used to prepare beautiful teas not only for the cricketers but also for the families who came down to watch. She'd bring out a tray with a cloth and tea cakes and sandwiches beautifully prepared and it was quite a highlight of the week.'

Normanby Park Cricket Club was formed in 1900, and by the 1930s, had become one of the strongest club sides in Lincolnshire.

'Oh we'd beautiful games, no doubt about that. There's been as many as over 400 runs scored in an afternoon, same when you was away.'

Matches were friendly fixtures of one innings duration with no over limits, captains declaring when they thought fit. The players either lived in Normanby Village or were local farmers or professional people but a handful of others also came from places such as Alkborough and Scunthorpe in the immediate vicinity. Hockey was played in the Winter months but not football.

Members of the Sheffield family have been keen cricketers at various times, especially Major Reginald Sheffield who captained the Club after the Second World War. They also maintained the ground and facilities free of charge. In the early years, the ground was mowed and rolled by horse, and there was even a stable behind the pavilion. There was also a grass tennis court. Other tennis courts used by the family were situated adjacent to the eastern wall of the kitchen garden.

If you became a Club member you were expected to take playing seriously,

'When you joined, you'd more or less got to play every week. I mean it was either a death or a wedding or something like that if you couldn't play. That was sport in those days.'

In 1926, a junior team called the Normanby Park Colts was formed by a Scunthorpe solicitor called George Davy, who lived in Normanby. His idea was to provide a nursery side for the senior Normanby Park teams but also and more importantly to give local boys the opportunity to play cricket and be expertly coached. They rapidly became a useful side and, in their inaugural season, won seven of their eleven matches. These were against a variety of local school and boys' teams and teams from as far away as Lincoln. The first captain was Fred Sutton, who succeeded his father as the Burton village saddler and went on to have a long and distinguished career in the Normanby Park First XI.

A charming annual event held at the ground between the Wars was the 'Normanby Park Cricket Week'. This was a festival similar to others held at country houses up and down the country. An example today is the Duke of Norfolk's festival at Arundel Castle in Sussex at the beginning of the cricket season.

In 1926, the Festival took place in the second week in August and teams included invitation teams such as 'Lady Sheffield's XI' and 'Mr. George Sheffield's XI'. The latter, composed of Eton schoolboys, played the newly formed Normanby Colts, eventually losing by an innings and eleven runs! Thomas Sumpter's son recalls,

'Father as a young man was a very keen cricketer and soccer player. His uncle, a chap called Joe Kitchen who played centre forward for Sheffield United and for England, was a professional cricketer and he used to spend a lot of his Summer being invited to go to these weeks by various landed gentry to bolster the side. Uncle Joe used to take father along with him and father always said that the best cricket he ever played was in these cricket weeks.'

Today Normanby Park Cricket Club is still a flourishing institution. The ground has grown in size boasting a new pavilion, and it is still a lovely place to play and enjoy sport.

The road outside the main gates of the Hall looking towards Normanby Village in the early 20th Century.

Normanby Village from the east c.1905-1910. The first cottage on the right was always the residence of the head gardener at the Hall.

NORMANBY

Head gardener Ernest Allen's cottage garden in Normanby Village c.1900-1910. He can be seen on the right of the photograph.

Mr. George Campbell the Normanby dairyman with his milk float , taken in the Village during the inter-War period.

Normanby Village street looking east towards the Hall and Park in the early years of the 20th Century.

Normanby School in 1914.

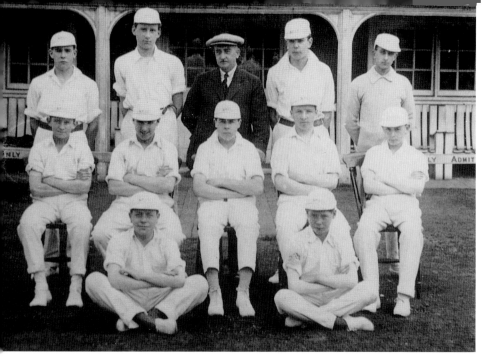

Normanby Park Colts in their second season in 1927 taken outside Normanby Park cricket pavilion. The gentleman in the centre wearing the flat cap is their coach Mr. J. Naylor.

MONDAY, AUGUST 9th, 1926.
Normanby Park Colts v Mr. George Sheffield's XI.
[Twelve a side.]

MR. GEORGE SHEFFIELD'S XI.

	FIRST INNINGS.		SECOND INNINGS.	
J. P. Henderson	c Naylor, b Gilliatt,	1	run out,	0
M. Behrendt	b Naylor,	1	run out,	10
G. Lloyd	b Naylor,	7	c Dunn, b H. J. Dain,	4
H. Gough	run out,	0	b Dunn,	0
C. Atkinson-Clark	c Naylor, b Gilliatt,	0	c Sutton, b Dunn,	1
E. Urry	b Gilliatt,	1	c H. J. Dain, b Naylor,	30
G. Sheffield	c Brown, b Gilliatt	17	c H. J. Dain,	0
J. Sheffield	b Naylor,	0	c R. W. Dain, b Naylor,	3
B. Mylne	c Brown, b Naylor,	0	b Naylor,	0
D. Walshaw	b Naylor,	0	c Dunn, b Gilliatt,	4
R. Gough	not out,	1	run out,	0
J. Walshaw	c and b Naylor,	1	not out,	0
Extras	...	2	Extras	3
	Total	31	Total	55

THE COLTS.

R. Wynne	c Lloyd, b Behrendt,	0
W. E. Dunn	c G. Sheffield, b Urry,	14
T. B. Gilliatt	b Atkinson-Clark,	17
J. N. Naylor	b Atkinson-Clark,	1
F. Sutton	not out,	31
H. J. Dain	b Urry,	0
R. W. Dain	c and b Urry,	0
W. Hall	b Urry,	0
E. H. Dain	b Atkinson-Clark	1
H. Wynne	c and b Urry	14
F. Brown	run out	0
W. Rowley	b J. Sheffield,	5
Extras	...	14
	Total	97

BOWLING.

COLTS.	FIRST INNINGS.	OVERS.	MAIDENS.	RUNS.	WICKETS.
Gilliatt		12	5	15	4
Naylor		11.2	5	14	6
	SECOND INNINGS.				
Dunn		10	2	11	2
H. J. Dain		9	3	24	2
Gilliatt		6.2	1	10	1
Naylor		6	3	7	2
Mr. SHEFFIELD'S XI.					
Atkinson-Clark		15	6	45	3
Behrendt		3	0	15	1
G. Sheffield		3	0	8	0
Urry		12	6	16	5
J. Sheffield		1.1	0	1	1

Page from a pamphlet containing the results of Normanby Park Cricket week matches held between the 9th and 14th of August 1926. It shows the details of the match between Normanby Park Colts and Mr. George Sheffield's XI.

NORMANBY IN BLOSSOM TIME

Come, let us sing a happy rhyme
Of Normanby at blossom-time ;
Laburnum, lilac, blood-red may
All breaking forth in glad array ;
The copper beech with branches wide,
And cherry trees dressed like a bride ;
While fluttering petals fall like snow
In Normanby, when blossoms blow.

Here twittering birds old carols sing
Afresh, with each returning Spring,
While garden plot and shapely bed
Blaze out in gold and white and red ;
Shy foxgloves, lupins, lilies sweet,
Quaint columbine and marguerite.
Oh! rare indeed the flower must be
That's not at home in Normanby !

The avenue's tall, shady trees
Fling out their pennants on the breeze
That bears along the merry tune
Of whistling waggoner-lads in June ;
And lovers there at eventide
Go wandering homeward side by side,
Wistful that wedding bells may chime
When Normanby's at blossom time.

A poem about Normanby Village written in 1946 by Edith Dudley.

Page Twenty-seven

END OF AN ERA

Throughout most of the first half of this century the owner of Normanby Hall and head of the Sheffield family was, of course, Sir Berkeley Digby George Sheffield Bt. J.P. D.L. He was born in Portland Place, London, on January 19th, 1876, and died on December 26th, 1946, aged 70. Succeeding his father, Sir Robert as 6th Baronet in 1886, he is perhaps the best remembered member of the family locally, renowned for his straightforwardness and good humour.

'I think he was very kind to everybody, and I mean there was no not talking to people, no snobbishness as far as the family was concerned, always very much concerned about the welfare of everyone.'

Sir Berkeley enjoyed a successful career in the Army and Diplomatic Corps, later entering politics. On the 19th May, 1904 he married Baroness Julia Mary de Tuyll. They had five children; Robert born in 1905, Diana born in 1907, Reginald born in 1908, George born in 1910, and John born in 1913.

During the last century the Sheffields were fortunate in discovering mineral deposits on their property which realised considerable amounts of money from ironstone royalties. This enabled Sir Berkeley to greatly extend the Hall between 1905 and 1907, doubling it in size. He then embarked on a career in politics, becoming the Unionist M.P. for Brigg between 1907 and 1910, and again, between 1922 and 1929 as a Conservative.

During the latter period he is remembered by a young housemaid working at a the Hall as,

'A proper country gentleman. And when I used to be taking the meal, the tray upstairs you see, he used to hear the door go, and he always used to come and meet me and take the tray off me when I had to take the tea up to the boudoir you see. And if he heard me coming with a log basket he used to come and help carry it for me.'

The impressive pedigree of the Sheffield family is illustrated by the fact that they were the original owners of Buckingham Palace. The story is told that Sir Berkeley Sheffield was invited to dine with King George V, and at the end of the evening the king said to him, 'Sheffield, have you noticed anything?'. 'No, your Majesty, I haven't'. 'Haven't you noticed that you're eating off your own plate!'. All the dinner service had the Buckingham crest on it. When the Sheffield family sold the house to King George III in the 18th century they had been Dukes of Normanby and Buckingham. They had evidently sold the dinner service along with the house, and this was still being used at the Palace!

Sir Berkeley was deeply interested in the affairs of Scunthorpe and was a popular Charter Mayor in 1936, when Scunthorpe became a Borough, something he regarded as a great honour. Perhaps the final word about Sir Berkeley and Lady Sheffield can be left to Harold Dudley, the curator of Scunthorpe Museum, writing in the *'History and Antiquities of Scunthorpe and District'* in 1930. Sir Berkeley was a generous friend to the Museum.

'Their benefactions throughout the district have been many and Sir Berkeley's own private tenants

on the Normanby estate esteem him for his ever present spirit of goodwill and kindliness. In every way, he and his wife have greatly enhanced the already honoured name of Sheffield.'

In 1949 a major change took place at Normanby when the large servants' wing was demolished and a sale of materials used in its construction was held in the stableyard. By this time Major Reginald Sheffield and his wife had become the new owners of the Hall following the death of Sir Berkeley Sheffield. The dining room was partitioned and the ground floor of the east wing converted into the new butler's pantry, kitchen and servants' hall. The former smoking room became the family's dining room and the billiard room, where Sir Berkeley had on occasions caught the footmen enjoying an illicit game of snooker, became a drawing room.

A young girl who started as a nursery-maid in the early 1950s on a wage of 25 shillings a week, but who was soon promoted to parlourmaid, later working as lady's-maid, recalls that the drawing room was where the

'Ladies retired when they'd had a dinner party. The gentlemen would stay with their cigars and brandy or whatever and the ladies retired into the drawing room to have their coffee you see, the men would stay behind in the dining room ... They had dinner at night, used to get the best china out, they'd all sorts of china in the safe, silver cutlery and glasses and it was all done very correctly. We had to learn to set the table correctly with all the cutlery. You know how cutlery is, you have so many different sets and three glasses and there used to be finger bowls.'

When guests stayed,

'They used to have big fires in the main hall, great big log fires, and big fires in the drawing room and in the library.'

The Hall was completely redecorated in 1951, including the library,

'The library, I remember them saying, you know how people talk, it cost a pound a roll to put that wallpaper on. I suppose in those days that was a lot of money.'

In the decade after the War, life at Normanby continued much as it had before the conflict, albeit with a reduced number of staff. The traditional 'London Season' had ended by this time and social life concentrated more on shooting, and occasions such as weddings, coming of age parties and the patronage of local events. In 1962 however, Major Sheffield decided to offer the Hall and Park to Scunthorpe Borough Council on a 99 year lease and moved to Sutton Park near York. The Borough Council took over at Normanby in 1963 and it has since been developed as a Museum and Country Park, thus opening a new chapter in its colourful and eventful history.

Sir Berkeley Sheffield taken during his first period of office as M.P. for the North Lindsey (Brigg) Parliamentary Division between 1907 and 1910.

Sir Berkeley Digby George Sheffield in the main entrance of Normanby Hall with Sir Edward Doughty M.P. on his right. In this photograph taken in 1908, he looks the epitome of the Edwardian country gentleman. Both were Members of Parliament at the time, Sir Edward for Grimsby and Sir Berkeley for Brigg.

Sir Berkeley Sheffield at his desk in his study in the east wing of the Hall.

Major E.C.R. Sheffield and Mrs. Nancy Sheffield with their son Reginald outside the garden entrance to the Hall in the 1950's. This photograph was used in a family Christmas card.

A unique phtograph of Normanby Estate staff past and present taken outside the Hall in 1967. This was during celebrations to mark the 21st birthday of Sir Reginald Sheffield.

ACKNOWLEDGEMENTS

Scunthorpe Museums Service would like to thank the following people for taking part in the Normanby Hall Oral History Project:

WILF ALLISON
GORDON ATKINSON
NORA BIRKETT
JOHN BRUMBY
RICHARD BRUMBY
DAVID COWLING
ESTER COWLING
ANN COX
ELIZABETH DENT
STANLEY FARNES
FRANK FLETCHER
DAVID GIBB
CHARLES GIBBONS
ANN AND ERNEST GOODBURN
ANNE HAWKINS
HOWARD HERITAGE
STEPHEN HILL
MEG HOLAH
FRANK AND RUBY HOLLINS
WILLIAM AND BARBARA HOLMES
NORMAN LILLEY
JOHN MARRIS
RONALD McGOVERNE
ROBERT NELSON
BRENDA RICHARDSON
IVY RICHARDSON
ROSELINA RIPLEY
RUBY SCOTT
KENNETH SILLS
ROBIN SUMPTER
FRED SUTTON

HARRY TAYLOR
FRANCES VERRAN
ALBERT AND LENA WALKER
WILLIAM WEST
IRVINE WHITELEY
BERNARD WINN
HILDA WOOLNOUGH

The Museum Service would also like to thank the following for their generous help:

Sir Reginald Sheffield
Lady Victoria Sheffield
Mr. G. Robinson
Mrs. R.J. Coulthurst
Mr. and Mrs. J.W. Kelsey
Mrs. G. Newell
Mrs. D.Newbury
Mr. S. Allen
Mr. C.Ketchell

Country Life Magazine
The Tank Museum, Bovington